What People are Saying . . .

From the Hood to Doing Good—real-life lessons from the young life of author Johnny Wimbrey. He gathers up his past adversities and formulates a new beginning. It's the experiences, not the years, that have surrendered wisdom to this young author, and from his adversity comes a success formula that will work for you too. "We all deserve a second chance," he says. Well, here is your chance to jump ahead in short order. Grab this book, read it tonight, and put the lessons into practice tomorrow!

Andrew Cauthen, Chief Marketing Officer
U.S. Health Advisors, Vice Chairman
American Millennium Corporation

In every generation, there are special people born who have the ability to touch and inspire the hearts and minds of others. I believe that Johnny Wimbrey is one of those special individuals. Johnny has "fire" in his spirit, which inspires others to transform their lives and achieve higher results because he has an amazing love of, a concern for, and belief in others. Plus, he possesses one of the most developed minds I have ever met. When you read *From the Hood to Doing Good*, you will see the essence of Johnny's soul on paper.

Al Johnson, President
Johnson Information Research

From the
HOOD
to Doing
GOOD

From the
HOOD
to Doing
GOOD

From Adversity to PROSPERITY
Through the Choices You Make

Johnny D. Wimbrey

WIMBREY TRAINING SYSTEMS. INC. PRODUCTIONS

Southlake, Texas

Published by Wimbrey Training Systems Inc. Productions
Southlake, Texas; an imprint of Westcom Press, Washington, DC

www.johnnywimbrey.com

Cataloging-in-Publication data for this book is available from the Library of Congress

Third edition, 2015

ISBN 978-1-938620-16-4

Wimbrey Training Systems Inc. Productions titles are available at special discounts for bulk purchases in the U.S. by corporations, institutions and other organizations. Custom publications with special materials and content can be developed for markets and events identified by those respective groups. For more information, please contact the publisher via www.johnnywimbrey.com.

10 9 8 7 6 5 4 3 2 1

VI

Dedication

To my beautiful wife, Crystal Wimbrey, my love and my best friend: I want to thank you from the bottom of my heart for all of your support.

Contents

Foreword

by Les Brown

It has been rightly said: It doesn't matter where you start out; what really matters is where you are going.

Johnny D. Wimbrey is a shining example of that reality. Using his life experiences, Johnny has proven if you have a willingness to do whatever is required and take the initiative to pursue your dreams, you can make some incredible things happen.

If you are willing to elevate your life beyond your circumstances, like Johnny has, and allow that to become your life mission, coupled with a strong belief in yourself and a power greater than yourself, the possibilities of reinventing your life and who you are now to who you can become are unlimited.

This book is designed to empower you with the secret process of success used by the rich and famous. Johnny takes you through a step-by-step proven method to transform your life and experience health, wealth, and happiness, which we all want. I found every chapter inspiring and enlightening, as I'm sure you will. Life for Johnny has, needless to say, not been easy. In this book he generously shares the road he traveled to escape mediocrity and poverty.

When Johnny addresses an audience, he encourages them to not allow their circumstances to determine their reality. He knows what it's like to be clobbered by life, thrown to the ground, and have dirt kicked in his face. But because of his faith and a determined unstoppable hunger to make something of himself, Johnny broke out of the hood . . . and is doing . . . I might add . . . very good, and the best is yet to come.

Johnny, you've done us proud, keep on making good stuff happen. The mark of greatness is upon you. This book will change your life; I guarantee it. This is Les Brown; Ms. Mamie Brown's baby boy.

Acknowledgments

*Each man is a hero and
an oracle to somebody.*

Ralph Waldo Emerson
Letters and Social Aims, 1876

Because this book reflects where I came from and who I used to be, and has been updated to include where I am now and who I am today, I gratefully acknowledge and thank those of you who have played important roles in my life.

First, I thank my Lord and Savior. Without a shadow of a doubt, I know without Him I would have been dead many years ago. For Christ I live and for Christ I die!

To my daughters, Psalms Noel Wimbrey and Hannah Joel Wimbrey, and my son, Honor Montrell Wimbrey: You are my why, and I pray for your success in everything that you touch.

To my father, a real man, Lawrence Eugene Wimbrey, Sr.: I'm proud of you for all that you have overcome and accomplished. I have always loved you and I always will.

To my mother, Phyllis K. Baron (Super Mom): I love you so much. You are a survivor and a fighter, and I owe my survival instincts to you.

To my stepfather, Tim Baron: You are the best thing that has ever happened to my mom, and I really thank you for *all* of your support and love.

To my brothers: Larry, I love you, and nothing will ever separate us. Keep your head up. Willie, if there were a thirteenth disciple, it would definitely be you (there will be streets named after you); thanks for being a friend.

And to my baby sister, Ronnietta: You are so special to me; please stay sweet forever. I love you!

A special thanks to Joyce Harris, for being a mother when my mother wasn't able to be there, and to Corey Harris, for accepting us and being a brother.

Big thanks to all of my in-laws, especially Momma-D for being one of my biggest fans.

To Pastor C. W. Gillespie and Dian Gillespie: I send my love and gratitude for sticking with me when everyone else gave up and counted me out as a loss as a youth. Sorry for all the headaches.

A special thanks to my entire family and loved ones, for all your consistent support.

To Jack and Regina Crane, "Papa and Momma Crane," whose love, patience, and support made all the difference in the world: Thanks for believing in me!

To everyone who has been there since Day One: Thanks! You know who you are. To *all* my partners in success, thanks for not expecting me or allowing me to be average! Thanks for all your love, support and motivation for me to succeed.

Introduction

*Insanity: Doing the same thing
over and over again
and expecting different results.*

Albert Einstein

I am extremely honored that over 125,000 copies of the first edition of *From the Hood to Doing Good* have been shipped to readers around the world. In the years since it was first published, many people have asked, "What is the HOOD, and how can *I* relate?"

Like many others across the globe, you will quickly discover that we *all* have experienced the HOOD. Whether you are a CEO of a Fortune 500 company, or a teacher, a student, an entrepreneur, or just beginning your journey into the real world, I have found that *everyone* can relate to the HOOD— Hazardous Obstacles Of Destruction.

We all experience life's adversities in some degree. The question is how you will choose to respond. Your response is not just your choice, it is your *responsibility*. You move from adversity to prosperity through the choices you make.

If winning is a possibility, why do some people perpetually choose to lose?

If you do the exact same thing today that you did yesterday, then your tomorrow will be just like your today. You must do something different to get something different!

Growth is a part of human nature, and change is inevitable. We were designed to mature and created to evolve. Our human nature wants to improve and grow—to increase. We find ourselves gearing up and mentally preparing for the journey of success, whether it be spiritual, mental, physical, or financial. We *all* were designed to thrive and crave the thrill of *increase!* We only become fearful to move forward and advance after we're introduced to the reality of life's obstacles.

When children make their first attempts at walking, they don't understand the "I can't" or the "what if" options. Although they fall down over and over again, they're not discouraged, they're determined. They're not contemplating other options; they don't know that other options exist. They're focused and ready for the next attempt. Could it be because they don't comprehend failure yet, or is it because they see walking as an achievable possibility?

At some point in our lives, many of us are introduced to the fear of failure. We begin to contemplate that success might not be our right when we learn that failure is an option. The thought of failure often paralyzes individuals from ever attempting to take the first step toward succeeding.

As a child, when you were asked what you wanted to be when you grew up, you may have said an astronaut, a police officer, a doctor, a lawyer, or possibly a dancer, singer, rodeo clown, or professional athlete. Your dreams had no limits because you had not yet been exposed to the reality of limitations.

I never heard a child say, "When I grow up I'm going to *try* to be a doctor." Children don't understand the word *try*. A child will look you square in the eyes and with unwavering confidence say, "I'm going to be a movie star." A child's formula for success is simple; here's the secret: "If they can do it, so can I!"

Children know that they can be taught to do anything.

Children don't understand the possibility of failure until someone introduces them to the fact that failure is an option.

Let's renew that childlike confidence. Never let a person define what's impossible for you to do!

Fear, in most cases, is a learned emotion. Although we were born with the natural ability to evolve and increase, our growth can be stunted when we are exposed to the giant opponent of every human being, the word **but.**

Listen to this: *I want to start a diet,* **but** . . .

When you use the word *but,* it cancels whatever you said before you used the word.

I love you, **but** . . .

When you use *but,* you cancel "I love you;" yes, the entire phrase.

In this book, you will learn how to cancel your fears, enhance your life, and feed your desire to succeed!

My personal story proves that if I can do it, anyone can. By all logic, I should've been dead a long time ago. I was not supposed to amount to anything; I was destined for failure. Success was not an option for someone with my past. People think someone like me does not deserve a second chance. There were only two places for men in my shoes: prison, or the graveyard . . .

BUT!

Chapter 1

Your Past Does Not Equal Your Future!

> *Where you've been has nothing*
> *to do with where you're going.*
>
> Anonymous

reat athletes prepare for competition through very intense training. They experience pain, sweat, and sometimes even tears, but their drive for success and the end results feed the desire to press on. Athletes understand that by lifting weights and exercising they may have pain, sometimes injuries, setbacks, and difficulties, but they also understand they are in the development and maturing process that prepares their bodies and minds for competition.

I have also lifted the weights of life and have been in mentally and emotionally rigorous workouts for years. It might surprise you, but I am deeply thankful for every hardship, every trial, and every burden. These personal experiences have molded me into the well-accomplished, relentless, and victorious man that I am today. I wouldn't change any of the experiences in my life for the world. Just as a champion's workout is more intense than the average, so was mine. I am a champion, and it's because of my emotional and mental growth from lifting my life's weights that I am here today. The best way out of difficulty is through it.

My earliest childhood memory was living in a battered women's shelter. You always hear that the first impression is the most important. It's true! Like it or not, we are ultimately labeled or prejudged by others' first impressions. It kind of seems unfair, doesn't it?

Well, think about it. Pause right now and take a second to remember someone you met for the first time who really impressed you. I mean, as soon as you saw this person, you immediately knew that he or she had life at its best. When they walked into a room, it lit up. I mean,

they had it going on! Now, I want you to think about
how you felt in the very moment you saw the person
who really impressed you. Did you feel alive, motivated,
energetic?

Now, switch to the complete opposite and think of
someone you met for the first time who really didn't
impress you *at all*. I mean, this person, in your mind,
was a pitiful sight.

When this pathetic soul came into your presence, the
whole atmosphere changed for the worse. You may not
even have known this person, but somehow, immediately it was obvious that he or she had issues.

Now, think about this person who didn't impress you at
all. What did it feel like? Did this person make you feel
down, negative, or drained? Did he or she affect your
mood, even if it was only temporarily?

The impression in meeting someone for the first time
has so much power or impact that it affects the way you
immediately characterize them. It also has the ability to
control your mind-set, your ability to think or feel good
or bad about them.

What about the impact of your first impression of *life*?

Life is Not Fair!

Life sucks! I think that would be a reasonable first impression of my life. When I was three years old, my mother ran for her life with my two older brothers and me. I mean, we literally ran out of our house in Fort Worth, Texas, with no shoes on and no destination.

The government shipped us to San Jose, California, and put us up in a battered women's shelter without my father having any knowledge of our whereabouts. It did not take me long to figure out that something was wrong with my life.

"Why do we have to mix powder and water together to make milk? I see everyone else pouring store-bought milk from a gallon jug."

"Why do we have to eat on the kitchen floor when everyone else eats at the kitchen table?"

"Why does our money come in a little book, and all the bills are different colors? Everyone else has green money and they can buy whatever they want. All we can buy with our funny-colored money is food."

I was in the first grade and we were just beginning to

experience a sense of stability in our lives when my mother decided to pack us up and move back to Texas. I was reintroduced to my dad, who was a stranger to me at the time. My mother and father never got back together, but because of my mother's financial problems at the time, my brothers and I were forced to live with my father.

After we spent several months getting settled in and finally becoming comfortable with our situation, my mother picked us up for what was supposed to be a short weekend, but, without my father's knowledge, she took us back to California.

I'd just finished the second grade when my mother told us that we would have to go back to Texas to live with our father, but this time she could not come with us. There are no words that can describe the fear and emotions that we three young boys went through. Our mother told us not to worry because she would be coming after us shortly.

We did not see our mother again for two years, and for months at a time I didn't hear from her and I was sure she was dead. When we got back to Texas I was forced to repeat the second grade and start all over, while living with a man I hardly knew.

"Life is not fair!" That could have been my attitude very easily. Maybe it's yours.

Let me ask you a question. Whoever told you that life was going to be fair?

This is the trap: We believe that life is dealt to us like a hand of cards, and whatever you get is all you get.

Well, I have some breaking news for you. In reality, ladies and gentlemen, you are in complete control of who you are, where you're going, and where you end up. *Your destiny is whatever you say it is.* Your destiny is wherever you see yourself going. If you don't see it or say it, there is no vision, and where there is no vision, people perish. **You are and will be whatever you say you are.** (We will discuss more about this in the next chapter, *Speak Life, Not Death*!)

In other words, where you come from does not necessarily mean that's where you will end up. Dan Mikals, one of my mentors, told me, "At some point in your life, you must flip the switch." What he meant was that until *you yourself* take action and flip the switch, there will be no change in your life.

It took me many years to finally realize this truth. For

example, all my young life people told me I was very talented, and that if I did not use my gifts it would be a waste. I was constantly in trouble as a youth, in school and in most aspects of my life, yet my teachers told me people would kill to have the talents I had.

I thought they were flat-out lying. I thought that's what teachers were required to say, that they were paid to flatter us. It used to really piss me off! I was tired of everyone telling me how talented I was, but how I was wasting my talents. I mean, they didn't know what I had been through. All through elementary school and junior high, I didn't dare slow down enough to think about my talents. I was just trying to survive the drugs, alcohol, deadly violence, and whatever else I had to go home to.

Could my teachers relate to a father jamming a gun in their faces, threatening to kill them, or wondering if their mother is alive because they haven't seen her in two years or heard from her in months? I did not want to talk about talents! I wanted to survive! How could anyone see such big talents in someone so small and yet hiding so much pain? How could they ever realize what talents I had?

The reason I got so angry is that they saw something in me I didn't even see in myself. It really hurts when you don't see "it" in yourself. My "it" was success—the talent to believe there was a chance that I, Johnny Wimbrey, could become great! I never thought about the future; all I thought about was surviving what I had to go home to.

What is your "*it*"?
Is *it* your past?
Is *it* your race?
Is *it* your sex?
Or is *it you*?

The Moment I Chose to Live

It was Sunday evening, January 31, 1993. I had just turned eighteen a couple days before, and I was watching Super Bowl XXVII's halftime show. The phone rang and I answered it. One of my friends was on the line, calling to let me know that one of our homies from the hood was shot and killed the night before at a local bowling alley. Although I had had friends who had been murdered, when I got this message I went numb.

Not only was I good friends with Mookie, the dead man, I also grew up with the person who killed him. These two individuals represented two different gangs in our area. We all went to school together, and we had all been fighting each other since the seventh grade.

In my mind, the real war had just begun. I was very angry and had every intention of retaliating for my friend's murder, but the gang all agreed to wait until after his funeral.

Destiny is not a matter of chance,
it is a matter of choice;
it is not a thing to be waited for,
it is a thing to be achieved.

William J. Bryan

God works in mysterious ways! Friday, February 5, was the night of Mookie's wake. All of us in the gang brought our guns to the church, prepared for anything. Somehow his mother found the strength to make her way to the microphone to speak to us. We were unprepared for what she had to say.

She told us the story of a recent conversation she had with her son. She said that Mookie, or Chris, as she called him, had come to her a few weeks before, and he told her he was tired of running, that he was finally ready to live right. Then Mookie gave his gun to his mother because he was serious.

None of us knew about this incident, but when we

looked back, we realized there had been something different about Mookie lately. I saw the tears in his mother's eyes and all the pain she was going through, and I was amazed to hear her express her forgiveness to the young man who had killed her son.

I had an epiphany! Who was I to seek revenge for a friend who had been murdered if his own mother had already found forgiveness?

That night I gave my gun to the preacher. I told him I didn't want to live like that anymore, and I asked for help. I prayed that night for God to send someone into my life who would help me stay focused on doing what was right. I needed a reason not to go back to the streets.

The very next day at the funeral, I met Crystal, the young lady who would become my wife several years later. I remember thinking to myself that this girl is too innocent for me, and I was nowhere near her type. She lived in a middle-class neighborhood and had a very loving and supportive family. But we were immediately attracted to each other, and we became really good friends in a very short period of time.

I remember wanting to impress her and at the same time protect her from my past, present, and potential future. I valued our relationship so much that I began to change my lifestyle. Crystal gave me a reason and a purpose for wanting more out of life. So I began to act, talk, and dress differently around her. I never brought her to my side of town because I was afraid of her getting caught up in a dangerous situation.

As time went on, I began to think in a way I have never thought before. For the first time, I started to wonder about my future. I was afraid. I had never thought about the future; I lived one day at a time. As I began to think about the future—my future—I began to sweat; my heart raced; I was covered in fear. What did it have in store for me? Where was I headed, and what could I offer this young lady if our relationship got serious?

Up to that point, I had no idea what possibilities even existed. Thoughts of settling down and the possibilities of starting a family of my own terrified me. I did not want my future children's first impression of life to be a struggle as mine had been.

I had a change of attitude, and like Dan Mikals said, "You must flip the switch," so . . . I flipped the switch!

I was determined to be successful. I didn't care about my

past anymore. I had a new attitude, and I was not going to let anyone or anything stand in my way. And the first person I had to get out of my way was *me*!

Once I finally made up my mind that success was a must and failure was not an option, things began to change. At 18, I had a felony arrest, was a drug dealer, was part of a gang, carried a gun. By the time I was twenty, I was self-employed; I became a licensed independent insurance agent.

Insurance wasn't a logical job choice; because of my criminal record, I was turned down by the state insurance regulatory agency at first. I went to the judge who sentenced me, and he wrote a letter to the Texas Department of Insurance on my behalf, asking them to give me another chance. I don't know why they listened to him, but two weeks later, I received my license in the mail.

With hard work and determination, within six months I was one of the top agents in the nation with a national health insurance agency. By the time I was twenty-two, my first house was being built from the ground up. It was a two-story, four-bedroom home.

Within one month of closing on my new home, on July

27, 1998, I married Crystal, my long-time sweetheart. I then paid off all her debt and put her through her last year of college. We have been partners in everything ever since, raising our two daughters and our son while building a business together. It's not a 50-50 split, though—we each bring 100% to our relationship.

My goal for 2000 was to make a six-figure salary by the end of the year. By the end of May, I had earned over $100,000. I was five-and-a-half months ahead of schedule. I was interviewed on national radio stations and a popular television network as a young success story. Since then, I have conducted seminars around the nation, inspiring thousands and empowering the masses for greatness. I've written best-selling books, hosted my own Hollywood talk show, and been interviewed by the media countless times.

I don't say any of this to impress you, but to impress *upon* you—*if I can do it, anyone can!* Who would have ever thought that a biracial young punk ex-drug dealer who could roll a perfect joint by the time he was eight years old, whose earliest memory of life was marked by living in a battered women's shelter because his father was an abusive drunk, could ever gain the attention of tens of thousands of people from all walks of life and inspire them to greatness?

*Adversity causes some men to break,
others to break records.*

William Arthur Ward

Why would someone listen to me? I don't have a college degree or a prestigious background that would qualify me to speak before thousands. I asked myself this question hundreds of times until I was becoming my own worst enemy. Then, one day, I read the quote that has changed my life forever: *"Adversity causes some men to break, others to break records."*

I began to say it to myself, and I still do every day, adding another sentence. *"Adversity causes some men to break, others to break records. And I am a record breaker."* As soon as I started to say that to myself, I began to break records. Are you a record breaker? Do you want to be?

What I tell myself may seem a little arrogant, but if you believe that, you are your own greatest enemy. There is nothing wrong with confidence. *Those who don't understand the difference between arrogance and confidence will always be intimidated by confident people.*

The fact is, if you don't believe in your own greatness, no one else will. How else can you be great unless *you* believe that you are? And how else can you believe you are unless you're confident in what or who you say you are?

I once heard someone say, "The best way to predict your future is to create one." I'm living proof that this statement is true.

God doesn't make mistakes; we do. The question is not "Have you made mistakes?"

The question is, "Will you get back up?"

Your past does not equal your future. In spite of your past, you still have infinite possibilities. Where you've been has nothing to do with where you're going! The reason it's called the past is because it's behind you. Although your past has everything to do with who you are today, it's not necessary to consult your past to determine your future.

The best way to predict your future is to create one.

What are *you* creating for *your* future? Take control! You are a record breaker!

.

Chapter 2

Speak Life, Not Death!

---

*Death and life
are in the power of the tongue.*

Proverbs 16:21 (King James Version)

The above proverb is an exceptionally true and powerful statement. The very words that come from your mouth will produce either life or death.

Watch what you say! Whatever you say will become your reality. If you say you're stupid, you will be stupid; if you say you're smart, you're smart. Whatever you say you are, that's what you are and will be. You literally become whatever you say and believe you are.

If you say you can; you can;
if you say you can't, you can't.
Either way, you're still right.

Henry Ford

In some of my seminars, I teach that there's always a positive way to say something negative. For example, instead of saying "I'm sick," tell people you're in the process of being healed. *Never* tell another person that you're broke! Say instead, "My finances are in transition." I truly cringe when I hear people say, "It's just my luck," or "with my luck . . . ." To me, when you say those negative words, you don't believe there's any possibility for good things to happen to you.

There's nothing wrong with expecting great things to happen to you. You are worthy. Nothing can hold you back but you yourself.

I remember the first time I heard someone say, "Look in the mirror and tell yourself you are great." I thought to myself, this dude must be nuts! He wants me to look in the mirror and say positive things to myself? I was Mr. Cool, and to me, looking in the mirror and talking to myself didn't come across as too cool.

Not too long after that, though, I was at home brushing my teeth in front of the mirror and I began to think about what the man had said. I thought, "OK, I'm home alone, no one will ever know." So I began to wonder, "What can I say to myself that would be positive and self-affirming?" Me being Mr. Cool and playing around, I looked dead into the mirror and said, "Johnny, I love you."

Instantly, the most incredible thing happened to me. I began to cry like a baby. I mean, here I am, home alone, crying with no explanation. At first I tried to compose myself and play it cool. And then I said to myself, "Hey, I'm home alone; Johnny, let it go." I must have cried for fifteen minutes, with no comprehension of why I was crying.

I was twenty-four at the time, and what really happened at that moment didn't hit me until a few months later. As a man, I wasn't used to hearing another man tell me, "I love you," because I had never heard it from my father.

My biggest revelation was this: Until that moment I never really understood what it meant to love yourself. I had thought it was selfish to love yourself, but in reality, how can you truly love someone else unless you learn to love yourself first? I realized that if no one else said great things about me, I must say them to myself.

Well-ordered self-love
is right and natural.

Saint Thomas Aquinas

Since that realization, every day of my life I take a moment to affirm myself. These are things that I tell myself on a daily basis: I am a great husband; I am a wonderful father; I am highly blessed and highly favored; I am the head and not the tail; I am above and not beneath; I'm blessed when I come in and I'm blessed when I go out; I will speak life; I will empower masses for greatness; I am a world changer; I am a man of integrity; my words have power to move mountains; I am a record breaker; and anything I put my hands to will prosper.

There are some who will think that these practices are arrogant. But as I stated in chapter one, people who don't understand the difference between confidence and arrogance will always be intimidated by confident people.

You must believe that you are a success before success can manifest itself in your life. It's literally impossible for you to believe it unless you physically say it and hear it.

Let's clear up some misperceptions. People often mistake money for success. The world teems with rich people who haven't experienced or tapped into the true definition of success. Money will magnify any and *every* habit that you have. That can be a good thing and that can be a bad thing. If you have a habit of donating money to charities, chances are when your wealth increases, your donations will increase too. If you have a drug habit and your money increases, chances are your drug use will expand also.

The love of money is said to be the root of all evil. Don't let the love of money detour you from your success. Use money as a tool for good, a tool for giving back, for others, for your family and friends. But don't let it be the end-all of your existence.

How will you handle your success when it comes? You need to be prepared, and you need to write those preparations down so that they are in your face every day. Who knows when you may need to be reminded?

The Mission Statement

I believe that it is paramount to write down your vision. You need to make it plain, because where there is no vision, people perish. In our home, we have a mission statement that sets forth the vision for our home and the legacy that we will leave.

Our mission statement says that we will speak words of life by encouraging, motivating, and empowering the masses for greatness. We will strive to accumulate great wealth through hard work and determination, while strategically employing our money to work for itself so our children's children will have a great inheritance that will in turn make them destined for greatness.

I charge each and every person who is reading this book—whether you're young or old, male or female, black or white or Asian, it doesn't matter—to write your vision and make it plain. Speak it loudly and with conviction at least twice a day, and see if what you speak with conviction comes to pass.

Read this aloud: **I will do today what others don't, so I will have tomorrow what others won't.**

Again: **I will do today what others don't, so I will have tomorrow what others won't.**

Again: **I will do today what others don't, so I will have tomorrow what others won't.**

Ladies and gentlemen, it is very simple. If you say you will, *you will*, and if you say you won't, *you won't*. Take control of every word that comes from your lips, and take every negative thought captive. Separate yourself from negative people, and attach yourself to successful, positive, energetic people who speak life into you.

Les Brown once stated that the only thing more important than saying, "I can," is saying *"It's possible!"*

I have always been the type of person to think, "If someone else can do it, so can I." I know that if it's possible for someone else, it's possible for me.

You are a possibility! Reach high, dig deep, press through, and say it's possible!

You Can Do *All* Things!

There's nothing to fear—you're as good as the best,
As strong as the mightiest, too.
You can win in every battle or test;
For there's no one just like you.
There's only one you in the world today;
So nobody else, you see,
Can do your work in as fine a way:
You're the only you there'll be!
So face the world, and all life is yours
To conquer and love and live:
And you'll find the happiness that endures
In just the measure you give;
There's nothing too good for you to possess,
Nor heights where you cannot go:
Your power is more than belief or guess—
It is something you have to know.
There is nothing to fear—you can and you will.
For you are the invincible you.
Set your foot on the highest hill—
There's nothing you cannot do.

Author Unknown

Winning With Words

Reneé Hornbuckle, founder of The Women of Influence Conference, paraphrased Dr. James Dobson's powerful concept in a seminar: "It takes seven positive comments to cancel one negative comment." To me, that was a very powerful and chilling revelation.

Think about it for a second. Can it be true? Could it really be that simple? Does this mean that anyone could literally take control of his or her destiny by canceling every negative statement or comment with seven positive ones? Could this assertion be challenged for validity? Sure, it could. I will be the first to tell you that I found it hard to believe. I'll also be the first to tell you that while researching whether this was a myth, I became a firm believer in Dr. Dobson's theory.

You have to understand that I am a realist. So it was very important to me to find out whether this statement, this declaration, if you will, had some truth to it. I began to look for someone to tell me something negative. I purposed in my heart that for every negative report I received, I would cancel it with seven positive ones. I was determined, I was ready for war, I was hungry, and I wanted someone to tell me what I couldn't do. Tell me I'm not the man for the job, tell me I'm not good enough!

*People who say it cannot be done
should not interrupt those
who are doing it.*

Anonymous

You know, it's amazing, but I didn't have to look hard or long. There's always someone willing to kill your dreams and hold you back.

I remember this as if it were yesterday. I was very excited because I had found the home that I wanted to build. I was only twenty-one, and I had never owned a home before, and I wanted a two-story, four-bedroom house with a two-car garage and two-and-a-half baths.

How many of you know that you can't share your dreams with everyone? I showed the plans to a couple who I really cared about, and I knew they were going to be happy for me. With excitement, with my chest puffed up with pride, I handed the plans to them and said, "Look at the home I'm going to build." As they looked at the plans, they slowly peered up at me, and with a simple smirk they said, "This house is too big for you; it's not realistic. You don't have any credit, and it would be better if you started out with a starter home."

Ladies and gentlemen, that's all I needed to hear. The trumpets began to sound, and it was time for war!

I got in my car, and with fire in my eyes I told myself, "This is my house; nothing will stop me from getting this house. The land is mine, and I will build. I will not be denied!

I drove to the land I had chosen, and I began to march around it seven times as I declared, "This is where I will build my home! I will not be denied!" Every time I said this, I began to believe that nothing could stop me from getting that house. I was invincible and ready for adversities. I saw myself living on this land, and I began to speak of the land as if it were already mine. I literally forgot the negative comments I had heard, and I began to believe that there was no way possible I could ever be denied that house.

The person who sends out positive thoughts activates the world around him positively and draws back to himself positive results.

Norman Vincent Peale

It wasn't until several months later, after being approved for the loan with the best interest rate possible and several thousands of dollars' worth of upgrades for free, that I remembered that someone had said I couldn't do it. I'm telling you, I forgot! I literally canceled the negative comment by replacing it with a repetition of positive reinforcements. Dr. Dobson's theory worked!

It's very important to me that you understand my friends didn't mean to hurt me when they said I couldn't possibly get the house I wanted. They were speaking from their own experience, and in their opinion, they were trying to help me. It would have been very easy for me to accept their reality because they were speaking from personal experience.

Who was I to tell them that they were wrong? I had never bought a house before; they had. I was barely 21. I'd never even considered building a house a year before and had never built one; they had. Reflecting back, it seems the reasonable thing to do at that time would have been to submit to their wisdom because, as I said before, *they were speaking from experience.* However, I had already purposed in my heart and was prepared for any negative comment. I mentally equipped myself to counteract any such comment and cancel it with seven positive ones. I had no idea that the situation would be so extreme, but I'm glad it was.

Reneé Hornbuckle's message emphasized that whatever you say the most about yourself becomes your reality. Seven is thought to be the number of perfection. What a beautiful thought and belief: If you simply say I can seven times to cancel every time someone says you can't, you become unstoppable!

People you know will always project their experiences and try to convince you that they're your reality as well. I dare you to promise me that the very next time you receive a negative comment, you will cancel it by saying seven positive ones.

You may read this and say it is a myth, it's crazy, it won't work; it is not real. I'm here to tell you it's real!

It's real!

    It's real!

        It's real!

            It's real!

                It's real!

                    It's real!

Chapter 3

Friends or Foes?

A friend is someone who knows all about you— and still loves you.

Elbert Hubbard

There are many ways to define a true friend. This chapter is not geared to give you a traditional definition of either *friend* or the other side of the coin, *foe*. You see, when I say friend or foe, I'm speaking of much more than just a human being.

If I ask you for your definition of the word *friend*, most likely you will answer along the lines of "a person that I can share my deepest desires with," or "someone who's going to be there through thick and thin."

A friend is one who believes in you when you have ceased to believe in yourself.

Anonymous

If I ask you for your definition of foe, you'll probably say, "an enemy" or "someone who's against you." You're right! Those are both fair and accurate definitions.

But now I will challenge you for a second. Let's be practical. Let's go back to the basics. Let's expand our traditional mindset and think outside the box. If I ask a group of five-year-olds, "What's a friend?" most will give me simple answers: "someone who helps people," or "someone I like."

If I asked those same kindergartners "What's an enemy?" I can almost guarantee they will say, "someone who's bad," or "someone who hurts people."

Wow! Isn't it fun to reflect back on the basics?

These children can't imagine having a bad person as a friend, or declare that someone who hurts people is our best friend because he's always there through thick and thin. Those people are supposed to be our foes! Our childhood innocence seems to be a misplaced treasure of revelation. Sometimes the minds of the young and innocent hold the true answers to the obstacles and cancers of life.

*A true friend is someone
who is there for you
when he'd rather be anywhere else.*

Len Wein

Vince Lombardi, who was named Coach of the Century by ESPN, had a special back-to-basics short talk with his Super Bowl champions at the beginning of every football season. He'd hold up a football and say, "Gentlemen, this is a football." Even though he was talking to professional football players, Coach Lombardi understood that in order to *stay* brilliant, you must *be* brilliant with the basics. I believe if we are to experience true victory over our greatest struggles and battles, we must get back to the basics.

As I said before, a friend or foe can be much more than a human being.

A friend is some*thing* or some*one* that helps you become everything God created you to be. A friend is any person, any place, or anything that's pushing you toward your destiny.

A foe is some*one* or something that tries to stop you from getting there. A foe is any person, any place, or anything that's holding you back from your destiny.

> *Never explain—*
> *your friends do not need it*
> *and your enemies*
> *will not believe you anyway.*
>
> Elbert Hubbard

Yes, a friend could be a person, place, or thing that's building you into being a better person. Do the places where you hang out the most help build you into a better person? What do you listen to? Does that help build you into a better person? Who do you socialize with, and do these people help you become a better person? Where do you spend your time on the internet? Are you watching what will make you a better person?

Is it possible that you surrounded yourself with your enemies, and you actually spend much of your time being entertained by the poison your true foes spew out?

This is where it gets hot, and if you can't stand the heat, you might want to get out of the kitchen. I'm serious. This may be the point where you want to close the book. It's self-inventory time! We are going to go face-to-face with who you really are. Everyone will not be able to handle this, but for those of you who want to become a better person, you're at the right place at the right time.

Identify Your Foes

You cannot fight your enemies if you don't know who your enemies really are. I learned the hard way that I must surround myself with people who celebrate me, not people who tolerate or are jealous of me.

One day, I was driving down the road, and I saw a BMW roadster coming the other way. When it flashed by me, I knew I had to have one. A week later, I bought my own. I was so excited, I drove that bad boy right off the showroom floor. I was more than da bomb, I was the explosion after da bomb! I wanted to share my excitement with other people, but I still remember how I was challenged to come up with more than one person who would be genuinely excited for me.

I know that Crystal is a true friend, so I called my wife first. She was so proud of me. She celebrated me, and that made me feel good. I began to show a few family members and friends my new car, but very few of them said they were proud of me or happy for me.

I'm not saying that's all I was looking for, but even a dog needs a pat on the head every now and then. It didn't take a long time to figure out that there were two types of people in my life, and deep down inside I already knew which were which.

It's funny how we can sometimes subconsciously ignore the truth. It became obvious to me that deep inside I already knew with whom I could share my excitement and with whom I could not. With the few I could, I noticed I was myself when talking about how excited I was. With those I could not share my true feelings, I realized that I always had to apologize for my success and diminish it.

Some of you might be thinking, "What do you mean by 'apologize,' Johnny?" Well, instead of talking about the car, its handling, its features—all the reasons I really got it—I made it sound as though it was just a great deal. I implied I bought the car not because I was successful and earned it, but because it didn't cost *that* much more than an economy car. Didn't you know, they practically paid me to take it off the lot! I diminished the car, my excitement, and my accomplishments.

If you find yourself explaining why you have something, or how you got something with great value, and thus compromise and downplay your success, then you are talking to a foe.

Listen to me very carefully. I'm not saying that these particular foes are not your friends. I am saying they are not *true* friends. For some reason, when you're with these particular people, they do not allow you to be who you really want to be. That reality gives them the capacity to hold you back or slow you down on the road to your destiny.

Identify the Enemy in You!

I once had the honor and pleasure of hearing the NFL's great Deion Sanders speak at an event. He said something that night that was so profound, it has literally changed my outlook on life forever. Mr. Sanders said that the enemy is "In-a-Me"!

This was my eureka moment, a time for self-inventory. Did I really possess the capacity to be my own enemy? Could I be my own foe? Could I be the enemy, my

"In-a-Me"? After a serious evaluation of self-character analysis, I have come to the following mind-boggling conclusions.

It is a man's own mind,
not his enemy or foe,
that lures him to evil ways.

Buddha

It is my belief that building character is a never-ending process. During every moment of your life, down to this very second, your character is constantly evolving. You are now, and forever will be, in a constant character-building state. It is humanly impossible to stop the process of character building.

All you see, smell, hear, taste, or touch during your everyday experiences builds your character. Although you may not be able to stop character building, you can *control* what's building your character. Everything you watch, everyone you entertain, and everywhere you go builds the content of your character, for better or for worse. You can and must control that.

You may be the life of the party, someone everyone loves, and people may say you are a person of great character. That's what the people see, and that's wonderful, but the true definition of character is different.

Character is who you are when no one else is around to see your actions.

When you're home alone and nobody is there to judge you, what do you find yourself doing? When you're driving down the street, all alone in the car, what are you thinking about?

Whatever the answer is, that's who you really are. Are you satisfied with this answer? If you are, that's great; if not, what are you willing to do about it?

I remember when I was a kid watching Saturday morning cartoons, a little cartoon character-looking thing used to come on during commercials and say, "You are what you eat." Of course, this commercial promoted the consumption of healthful foods. In a nutshell, the commercial simply stated that healthful food equals a healthy body.

This is also true with character. Your character is developed according to what you consume or what consumes you.

What do you watch on TV? What music is in your ears? What do you do on your iPad or laptop? Do you have healthy social habits? These are all questions that you should ask yourself (and answer) as you do your self-inventory.

> *Avoid cynical and negative people*
> *like the plague.*
> *They are killers of potential.*
>
> **Rick Pitino**

The things that entertain you the most and the things that you hate the most, they are who you are. Is this beginning to make sense?

Let me give you an example. For instance, I hate being around negative and complaining people. It literally makes my flesh crawl to hear people complain while they allow petty situations to master them. You know why? Because of who *I* am. I'm a positive individual, and I love to be around positive people. I am an encourager, I love to encourage people, but negative, complaining folk love to share their misery. Negative people drain me, and I understand that about myself, but if I still choose to be around negative people, this makes *me* the "In-a-Me."

Why? Because I am responsible for understanding the difference between the things that build me up and those that tear me down. And once I understand this fact, I must hold myself accountable for the persons, places, and things I choose to entertain.

Once you identify the entities in your life that appear to be your foes, you had better make an uncompromising decision immediately to cut them off. I don't care who or what they are, once you identify them, let them go. The moment you begin to compromise this decision, that's the moment you become the In-a-Me.

You might ask, "What if it's someone or something that I really care about, or a family member? Johnny, are you saying that I should have nothing to do with them?" No, but what I am saying is that there needs to be a season of separation. You can love them from a distance. (Please note, this does not apply to your spouse. If your spouse is your foe, that's a whole other book.)

You have to understand that this season is for *you*. This is *your* time for developing a passion toward creating a better you. In order for you to tap into your destiny, you must go through a season in which you make it *all* about you. This is your time to really evaluate who is *for* you and who is *against* you.

I struggled big time with this! In high school I was Class Favorite, Most Likely to Be Remembered, and Homecoming King. My point is, I had a lot of friends who I felt really close to, but after high school I began to focus on other things instead of just hanging out. I didn't want people thinking that I thought I was too good or that I wasn't down with them anymore. I did not want to separate myself from my homies who I used to drink and get high with. I mean, these were my Day-One Homies!

And what about my crazy family? "I know they're a little wild," I told myself, "and they are always talking about other folks and gossiping, but they don't mean any harm. I can still hang out, I just won't do what they do, and I won't talk about the things they talk about." Yeah, right! If you're thinking like I was thinking, then you are setting yourself up for a fight you will not win. It's that simple!

A Do or Die Situation!

When I became twenty-one, I was determined I was going to walk the straight and narrow. At this point I was engaged to Crystal and doing very well financially. I felt it was time to take it to higher level spiritually, so I rededicated my life to God. I threw away every negative CD and movie that I owned and began to listen to things that built me up, not tearing me down. I surrounded myself with information and put myself into situations that stretched me to become better.

But I was not yet ready to give up my Day-One Homies. I believed that our relationships and the time that we spent together did not have to decrease in order for me to increase. Boy, was I wrong!

I remember it like it was yesterday. One Sunday evening during the summer of 1996 my homies and I were kicking it once again, but this time I was different. I wasn't drinking; I wasn't getting high; I was just there for the fellowship. A little time passed, and I rationalized, what the heck, one drink won't hurt. To make a long story short, by the end of that Sunday night I found myself running for my life while being shot at with a street assault rifle.

Despite every good intent, I got into a confrontation with another guy. I even tried to walk away and get into my car, but he obviously thought I was going to my car to get a gun. So he ran to his car, popped his trunk, grabbed this huge gun, and began to chase me down while frantically shooting at me. I dove behind my car and curled into a fetal position, convinced that this was it. I prayed to God to give me another chance! He did.

It's not fun being shot at from only about ten yards away. I should have died that night, but by the grace of God, I did not. To this day, those bullets cannot be accounted for, and my homies who witnessed the shooting say they don't understand how I didn't get hit. Association brings about assimilation.

Sigmund Freud said that you're a product of your environment. That night, I almost became a statistic of my environment. I made a foolish mistake: to trust and rely on myself instead of submitting to the reality that I must separate from some things and let them go. That night I almost died in the midst of being the In-a-Me.

That night was probably the longest ride home I've ever experienced. I had a lot to think about, and I had a lot of decisions to make. I began to understand that in order to get something different, you have to *do* something different.

I wanted something in life that I'd never had before, and I finally realized that in order for that to happen, I had to be willing to do something I'd never done before. I had to separate myself from any and all things with the potential to stagnate my growth toward achieving what

I consider to be the definition of success. I had to cut some things off. It was my season for separation.

I count him braver who overcomes his desires than him who conquers his enemies; for the hardest victory is over self.

Aristotle

When you finally are ready to find out who your foes are, I dare you to call for a season of separation. They will expose themselves. When you explain your motives, your true friends will celebrate you. You will discover your true friends, and you will clearly see your foes. A person, a place, or a thing could very well be both your friend and your foe. I am very happy to say my Day-One Homies supported me then, and they still do today. Thanks, guys!

Never feel guilty for wanting to better yourself. You should never sacrifice your success for a foe. True friends will not be intimidated by your passion and desire to increase your self-worth and net-worth. True friends will support you in your season of self-inventory, which becomes your season for finding the real friend within you.

A Time for Everything

There is a time for everything,

and a season for every activity under the heavens,

a time to be born and a time to die,

a time to plant and a time to uproot,

a time to kill and a time to heal,

a time to tear down and a time to build,

a time to weep and a time to laugh,

a time to mourn and a time to dance,

a time to scatter stones and a time to gather them,

a time to embrace and a time to refrain from embracing,

a time to search and a time to give up,

a time to keep and a time to throw away,

a time to tear and a time to mend,

a time to be silent and a time to speak,

a time to love and a time to hate,

a time for war and a time for peace.

Ecclesiastes 3:1-8 (New International Version)

Chapter 4

Mastering the Mind

We may have all come on different ships,
but we're in the same boat now.

Martin Luther King, Jr.

To Master or Be Mastered,
That Is the Question.

Nobody is immune to adversity, none are immune to temptation, and none are immune to life's trials and tribulations. Whether we'd like to admit it or not, we all fall short in life at one point or another. Every human being will experience the good, the bad, and the ugly. That's a reality of life. The questions are, what are you going to do about it, and when are you going to do something about it? In other words:

- When you get knocked down, how long will you stay there before you decide to get back up?

- When you receive bad news, how long will you ponder it before you move on?

- When you've been broken into pieces, how long will it take before you decide to put yourself back together again?

How Long Will You Decide to Be Mastered Before You Begin to Master?

They say confession is good for the soul, so let me come clean for a second. I, too, have a weakness. Yes, it's true! In the past, and sometimes even now, I struggle and have struggled with lost time. People who are not time-conscious frustrate me. I can't stand to be late, and I hate being unproductive. I value time because once it's gone, you can never get it back.

I programmed myself to think that way a long time ago. You may be thinking that it's a good and successful habit—and I agree—but anything you don't master will master you. Although I programmed myself to be a time-conscious individual, I never thought to prepare myself for situations that are potentially out of my control. This is where the problem lies. Good people can make drastically bad decisions when they're not prepared for an unpredictable situation that's out of their control.

You have a very powerful mind that can make anything happen as long as you keep yourself centered.

Dr. Wayne W. Dyer

Mastering the Mind

Some situations may seem very small and trivial to most people, but many small, trivial situations can and do escalate to very regrettable and drastic predicaments. I remember my first conscious decision to become the master in my personal battle against lost time. It was a beautiful, sunny day in Dallas, Texas, and I was happily driving my BMW Z3 roadster with the convertible top down. I was listening to good music; I was at peace and in the very best of moods. Then, as these things inevitably happen, I looked up and was shocked to see I had missed my exit. Instantly, I felt my blood pressure soar. I went from tranquil to furious in a matter of seconds.

I warned you this situation would sound trivial, but you must understand that by the time I could get back on course, I would have lost at least five or ten irreplaceable minutes. As you read this, you're probably cracking up, but I promise you, I am not exaggerating my state of mind. What's even funnier is that by this point, I had conducted seminars and self-help courses across the nation, and I had studied numerous different philosophies and personally participated in seminars on self-control.

Yet, here I was frustrated and out of control because I had missed my exit. As I exited the freeway and detoured through some back streets to get back on course, I began to think about something I had recently heard that was still fresh in my mind: *"If you want to get over a negative situation, begin to find positive things in your negative situation."*

So I figured, "What the heck? I have nothing else to do; let's see if it works." In the midst of my turmoil and frustration I began to look for positive things. My first reaction was that there weren't any, but then I began to look for simple things.

I remember it like it was yesterday. As I drove up to a red light I looked up. As a car was passing me, coming from the other direction, I noticed that the driver was smiling, and it was a world-class smile. I said to myself, "If I hadn't missed my exit I would never have been able to see that person smiling." Instantly, like magic, my frustration went away! Then I thought, "Man, this is cool." As the light turned green, I noticed that the signal's color wasn't your normal green, it was a fluorescent, brilliant green. And I thought to myself, "That's the prettiest green light I have ever seen. If I hadn't missed my exit, I would never have been able to experience this unique green light."

Now I must admit that all of this was totally out of character for me, but it worked. I began to feel excited, almost as if I was in a competition to find positive things. It was fun! I became the master of my own pet peeve. They say a mind is a terrible thing to waste, and I say it's terrible when you don't stretch and exercise yours.

Taking Control and Moving On!

Every individual holds the key to the God-given ability to consciously decide whether to master a situation or to be mastered by it. Every individual also has the ability to decide how long he or she chooses to master, or be mastered by, a situation.

In the previous chapter we discussed the importance of understanding that there is a time and/or a season for everything. It is very important that you also understand that every season will—and must!—come to an end.

As I conduct self-development training and seminars throughout the nation, it amazes me to find that only ten percent of most individuals' battles are caused by the situation. A full 90 percent of their battles are caused by their inability to move on and simply let go.

It has always been a personal struggle for me to watch people wrestle with situations that could disappear immediately if they would just simply let them go. It drives me crazy to see an individual allow himself to be mastered by a stupid situation. There are many great people from whom I purposely distance myself because they choose to be controlled by idiotic situations.

*Some of us think holding on
makes us strong;
but sometimes it is letting go.*

Hermann Hesse

For example, could a marriage come to an end because two loving individuals don't agree on whether the toilet paper should go over or under the roll? How can a woman be a loving wife and mother one moment and the next moment be booked for murder because of road rage?

Let's be real for a second! Toilet paper should never be the cause of any divorce, and road rage can never be the excuse for any murder. The simple fact is good people make stupid decisions when they choose to forfeit the right to master an obstacle or an adversity and become mastered by it instead. It is said that you can always measure the character of a man by the size of the obstacle it takes to overcome him. Good people become murderers every day—and good people are murdered every day—because individuals simply are not in control of their immediate emotions.

Think about it: How many people do you think are dead or in prison because of their middle finger or someone else's middle finger? Isn't it ridiculous to think that an outstretched middle finger could cause an individual's rage to escalate to the point of deadly force?

How hard would it be for most people to prepare or train themselves to never allow someone else's physical gestures to control them?

What and/or who has the ability to cause you to lose control and step out of your character? When you hear the words "lose control," it's probably a natural instinct to think of people who are literally out of their minds or crazy. We hear phrases all the time describing someone who loses control: "He really went off the deep end this time," "She just lost it," or "He just flipped." These are extreme examples, but we lose control every day.

No one can make you jealous, angry, vengeful, or greedy—unless you let him.

Napoleon Hill

It's a slippery slope. If you are not conscious of the fact that you are capable of losing control, you will adopt the habit of losing control. Once you have the habit of losing control, you've created a lifestyle of being out of control.

On the other hand, you can always regain control. Have you ever said ruefully, "I can't believe I just said that," or "I apologize for snapping like that?" These are good examples of how you can regain control.

Are you conscious of, and willing to recognize, where

you seem to be less in control? When and where do you master, and when and where are you being mastered? I believe if you practice mastering the basics—or what some would call the minor things in life—you are literally positioning yourself to avoid potential disaster.

I was once told that you should manage your weaknesses and master your strengths. I'm not saying that we will ever be successful at mastering all of our emotions and every situation, but I am saying that every successful step forward is a step toward being the master instead of being mastered.

Is it possible to be in control in a very intense and heated situation? Absolutely! Let me give you an example. Have you ever seen one of the NFL highlight specials, perhaps a Super Bowl highlight special without any editing, where you can actually hear what the football players are saying on and off the field? It amazes me to see a 300-pound man hit another 300-pound man on the field, see them slam each other to the ground and lie on top of each other, yelling and screaming insults at one another, close enough to taste each other's spit.

Then the referee blows his whistle and it's all over; they simply help each other up and walk away as if it never even happened. How can someone who is so revved up with intense energy and competitive emotions suddenly regain complete emotional, physical, and mental control?

The answer is simple. Obedience is better than sacrifice. The players are mentally conditioned by the coaches and staff to understand the consequences and penalties that come from uncontrollable behavior are simply not worth the risk.

You know what's really crazy? The exact same football player who has the ability and discipline to walk away from someone who's slammed him to the group, spit in his face and screamed insults, gets arrested the next week for being in a bar fight with someone who simply sneers that his team is lame.

How could this be the same person? Aren't real-life legal penalties more severe than NFL penalties? The real question is who's coaching and conditioning you to understand the adversities you will face in the real world, teaching you how to ignore and/or walk away from something that simply is not worth the risk?

Is it important to have mentors to coach you in every area of your life? (We will discuss more about mentors in the next chapter.)

We are God's only creation holding the gift of self-will. This means that we all possess the mental capacity to obey or to disobey, to lie or to be honest, to love or to hate, and the mental power to will ourselves to personal victory. As we learn to be the masters of our minds, we will begin to minimize our experiences of being mastered.

Not to have control over the senses is like sailing in a rudderless ship, bound to break to pieces on coming in contact with the very first rock.

Mahatma Gandhi

Chapter 5

The Psychology of Winning

Winning isn't everything,
but wanting to win is.

Vince Lombardi

Success leaves clues. There are no coincidences to winning. No one wins by chance or luck. Winners win because they want to win. Winners think about winning all the time.

Best-selling recording artist Nelly released an international hit, *What Does It Take to Be Number One?* The chorus line says number "two is not a winner and three nobody remembers." This album went straight to the top of the charts and made Nelly an international phenomenon. He wrote the song before he became number one in the public's eyes, yet he understood the concept of winning and attitude.

Winners eat, sleep, and breathe the concept of victory—of being number one. If you want to be in first place, you first must see yourself there. You must sell yourself on the fact that you are a winner and that you are number one, long before it's obvious to others. *Faith is the substance of things hoped for and the evidence of things not seen.* You must think like a winner in order to become one.

Terry L. Hornbuckle authored a book, *See Your Future, Be Your Future.* In his book he describes how important—and how necessary—it is for you to see your future before for your hopes, aspirations, and goals can become a manifested reality. You must believe without a shadow of a doubt that you deserve to win. And you must practice seeing yourself as the winner in order to be a winner.

> *Only a man who knows what it is like to be defeated can reach down to the bottom of his soul and come up with an extra ounce of power it takes to win when the match is even.*
>
> Muhammad Ali

Voted USA Today's Athlete of the Century, heavyweight champion Muhammad Ali mastered the psychology of winning. Long before Ali was the greatest fighter of all time, he told the world he was the greatest. Long before the world knew who he was, he told the local gyms that he was the greatest. And long before he became confident enough to become outspoken, he told himself he was the greatest. Ali first convinced himself that he was the greatest before he could convince anyone else.

The most important point to remember is: Not only is it necessary for you to continually remind yourself that you are a winner, it is mandatory for your opponent to see, hear, and feel your confidence in your own abilities to win. When your opponent begins to imagine you winning, half of the battle is already won.

---

*Other people's opinion of you
does not have to become your reality.*

Les Brown

Who is your opponent? Like your foe, your opponent can be anything or anyone who tries to keep you from coming out of the box.

My opponents are the odds that stand against me.

Society and statistics tell us that because I'm biracial, was born in the projects, lived on welfare, had an alcoholic for a father, and came from a single-parent home, that I supposedly will never control what ultimately will determine my future. According to society, I was supposed to have suffered emotionally at the hands of my peers because of my undetermined race; I am supposed to be struggling with alcoholic tendencies; I'm supposed to be socially and economically depressed; and my chances of ever experiencing a successful marriage are slim to none.

But my reality is very different. I could have had problems in school because of my race, but it was obvious that I was confident and very satisfied with who I was. In high school I was popular—in a gang, yes, but well-liked and accepted by kids in different groups. I don't have any dependency on alcohol, I live a very nice lifestyle, and my wife and I have been married happily for over seventeen years and we are still best friends today.

Listen very closely. Never let another's experiences become your reality! You are the only one who can officially determine who and what you will become. If you see yourself in society's preprogrammed box, that's where you will be. Never let anyone create your world for you, because they will always create it too small.

Am I a freak of nature? No! I am simply programmed by God to be the head and not the tail; to be above and not beneath anyone or anything. I was designed to win, and so I choose to walk with my footsteps toward my God-given right. I am mentally programmed to win. I am a record breaker! I am confident and not arrogant.

Everyone experiences hard times and struggles, but all winners have one thing in common: We don't like to lose.

Society has programmed us to think that if you're having trouble in your marriage, get a divorce. Almost all circumstances offer an easy way out, but the prize is given to the one who perseveres and finishes the race. Winners understand that through the thick and thin, we must win! Failure is not an option for winners. They say winners never quit. I can guarantee you a quitter will never be a winner!

A winner is someone who recognizes his God-given talents, works his tail off to develop them into skills, and uses these skills to accomplish his goals.

Larry Bird

A true winner also understands the importance of surrounding himself or herself with other winners. I have made it a personal goal in my life to constantly introduce myself to—and continuously surround myself with—people who stretch me.

All winners understand that you must get out of your comfort zone. You can't learn how to swim in shallow waters. Don't be afraid of the deep water. It's hard to move to a higher level if everyone around you is beneath you or on the same level as you.

I don't mean beneath you as though they are lesser people, because we know that we are *all* created equally. I mean, though, if you want to become an executive at your job, then you need to expose yourself to the mentality of executives. You can find one or more of the many people who are, or have been, where you are trying to go. Hang around winners and you will become a winner too.

The Importance of Having Mentors

Winners understand the importance of having mentors and they value them. Synonyms for the word mentor are teacher, adviser, tutor, counselor, guru, guide, or coach. Webster's dictionary defines the mentor as "a trusted counselor or guide." I have found that many people use the word "mentor" very loosely, though.

A mentor, first of all, is someone you know personally. You may admire a TV personality, but he or she is not your mentor unless you have personal access.

You choose your mentor; your mentor does not choose you. You may be approached by potential mentors who want to put you under their wings and guide you, but until you choose to go with them, these people aren't your mentors.

In addition, your mentor must accept the role, or he or she is not a mentor. A mentor should be able to correct you on the spot; you submit immediately and take heed of the directions offered you.

This is why you must choose your mentor, because the moment you don't willingly receive the advice, correction, or even open rebuke your mentor offers, then that person can no longer be your mentor.

*I'm a success today because I had
a friend who believed in me and I
didn't have the heart to let him down.*

Abraham Lincoln

In order to have a mentor, you must be a protégé! Synonyms and definition of the word protégé include dependent, student, disciple, one who accepts the charge.

You can have different mentors for different areas of your life. For example, you may have a physical mentor, a spiritual mentor, and a financial mentor. It's great if all of these are the same person, but it's not necessary.

How Do You Choose a Mentor?

Your prospective mentor:

- Has skill or experience in something you would like to master or experience. For example, you can play the saxophone, but your mentor is a superb sax player.

- Agrees to mentor you.

- Can tell you *no!*

- Has a lifestyle you respect in every facet.

- Maintains a completely honest relationship with you—both giving and taking, no matter what.

Mentors' jobs are to protect us. That's why it's very important that we be open and honest with them so they can tell, show, and give us everything we need that is in our best interests. True mentors will tell us what we need to hear rather than what we want to hear.

In the multitude of counselors there is safety.

King Solomon

Great mentors will inspect what they expect. In other words, they won't just tell us what to do; they will follow up or make sure we report our results. Mentors are not dictators but advisors who want us to succeed without sacrificing our integrity. Great mentors will never ask us to compromise good character to get to the top.

A great financial mentor will show you how to master your money, instead of your money mastering you. When your money tells you what to do, you are in trouble, but when you can tell your money what to do, you can and will experience true wealth.

I once read that open rebuke is better than hidden love. A great mentor understands that he or she must tell it to you like it is.

A great winner is also a great protégé who will apply the advice from the mentor that he or she chose. A mentor has every right to terminate a relationship with a rebellious protégé. Likewise, the protégé has every right to terminate a relationship with his or her mentor. Keep in mind, if you find yourself jumping from mentor to mentor because they are not what you expected them to be, chances are they are not the ones with the problems.

I will tell you from experience that there are plenty of times my mentors hurt my feelings, but remember, I chose them. Winners are not afraid of constructive criticism and understand that it takes iron to sharpen iron.

My wife Crystal and I are very blessed to have incredible marital mentors, Eben and Sara Conner, who hold us accountable to each other. We chose them; they did not choose us. They have counseled us on several occasions. I must admit that when I know I am right, I am very quick to call them to referee when Crystal and I are having intense fellowships (ahem, arguments).

I do confess that the majority of the times I call Eben and Sara so Crystal can get help (because I am right). Usually, I am the one the one getting the most help in the end.

Did you know that it is possible to deceive yourself? Deception would not be deception if it were obvious! You can be off track and not know it. And without correct navigation you will eventually crash.

Crystal and I know that Eben and Sara want us to win in every facet of our lives. And since they have our best interests at heart, we agree to submit to their wisdom. Wisdom is the application of knowledge. So when they share their knowledge, as their protégés we must apply their instructions, regardless of who is at fault.

A winner knows when to swallow his or her pride in order to resolve a higher cause and/or purpose. Winners understand that it is impossible to win by themselves.

Winners MUST Win!

Winners don't see success as an option; we see it as something that we must have. Average people want to win, but winners must win. While the majority of the world is talking about what they want to happen, the mentality of the winner is focused on what must happen. As a winner, you must be able to convert every one of your wants to your musts. When you want something, it's optional. But when you must have something, it's non-negotiable. Everyone *wants* to be successful; only a very few *must* be successful.

So how do you turn your wants into your musts? I've done seminars across the nation on this topic. When I ask the audience to give me a list of things that are a *must* in their lives, their answers are remarkably similar:

- be at work on time
- pay bills on time
- eat
- bathe
- buy groceries
- pay taxes

Then I ask them for their *wants* rather than their musts:

- eat healthy
- exercise
- go on vacation
- pray every day
- give to charity
- spend more time with the family

Typically, the things that most people see as a *must* are tied to negative consequences. For example, if you don't eat, you starve. Or if you don't show up for work on time, you will get fired. In other words, most people are programmed to perform in order to prevent immediate negative reactions. You have a *why* for all your musts.

OK, by now you should get the point. The only difference between the things that you *must* have or do and the things that you *want* to have or do is *you*. Your attitude determines your ability to succeed.

The majority of people do things because they don't want to suffer negative consequences.

Then there are the few who are driven by the thrill of success. These individuals understand that they must do today what others don't, to have tomorrow what others won't. These are the ones who have the ability to make things happen, and who are self-disciplined. It is very important to have a reason, or a *why*, for everything that you want.

Let me give you an example of a *why* I have for one of my wants. I must be successful because I *want* to leave an inheritance for my children's children.

When you find your *why* in everything that you want and become passionate with a burning desire for the end result, your wants will become musts. This is the reason that you must find a why for every one of your wants.

Wants + Whys = Musts

- I *must* eat healthy to live longer.
- I *must* exercise for energy and for good health.
- I *must* go on vacation because I work hard.
- I *must* pray every day to stay spiritually strong.
- I *must* give to charity to save lives.
- I *must* spend more time with my family to show my love.

My cause is bigger than I am, and because my wants have whys that are much more important than selfish desires, I am willing to fight for the end result. You must be willing to fight for the cause of your wants. It's hard to fight for something without a cause, so connect all of your wants to all of your whys so all of your dreams will come to fruition.

Chapter 6

Winners Make It Happen!

People of mediocre ability sometimes achieve outstanding success because they don't know when to quit. Most men succeed because they are determined to.

George Allen

W
hen people are on their deathbed, often their greatest regret is that they hadn't taken more risks in life. Isn't that mind-blowing? To think of all the things that one could regret, that one of the greatest would be wishing

that you had taken more risks. Not, "I wish I would have spent more time with my children and family," or maybe even "I wish I'd taken more elaborate vacations."

I wish I had taken more risks. How could not taking risks be so devastating? It took me a while before I got the revelation. I thought about this and it finally came to me. To take the risk requires but a moment; to not take risks becomes a lifestyle.

You have to do what others don't, to have tomorrow what others won't. Average people don't take risks, and average people live average lives.

He has not learned the lesson of life who does not every day surmount fear.

Ralph Waldo Emerson

Winners are not afraid to take risks. They understand if they are to win, they must go further than others are willing to go. Risk takers are more afraid of being average than they are of being ridiculed by spectators.

The only people who never fail are those who never try. You must be willing to go further than you've ever gone before. Dig deeper, push harder, and take more risks than you've ever taken before. And I promise you *will* go farther than you've ever experienced before.

He who is not courageous enough
to take risks
will accomplish nothing in life.

Muhammad Ali

A winner is not one who never fails, but one who *never quits*!

The ME Factor

What is the difference between your colleague who consistently makes Top Salesman of the Month and you? Why does your brother excel in athletics and you sit on the bench? Why are you on the outside looking in?

I call it the *You Factor*. You have the same abilities and just as much talent, but you haven't decided to work at it, or go for it, or train hard, or build your confidence, so *you* hold the reins. I want to twist those words and the ideas 360 degrees. We'll end up in the same place, but the phrasing will be different.

I have been very fortunate to meet tens of thousands of outstanding and incredible individuals from around the world through the seminars and trainings that I've conducted. I've been amazed by people who have overcome the most devastating adversities. Some smile and are full of energy. You would never know the obstacles and trials they've endured. Somehow these individuals were able to overcome life's hardships and understand how paramount it is to be victorious over any and all situations.

A woman whom I'll call Nancy told me her amazing story. She was virtually abandoned by her alcoholic mother when she was barely nine years old, and Nancy became the mother to her six-year-old and three-year-old brothers. She had to avoid the landlord, steal food, protect, comfort, and entertain her brothers. Her mother would show up at the apartment every so often with a different man in tow. After screaming at Nancy to clean up the mess, she'd disappear with her visitor into a back room. Some of the men gave the children money; some simply looked at them with a blank stare. Eventually, Nancy and her brothers went to live with their maternal great-grandmother. When she died, the children were sent to different orphans' homes.

> *The greatest glory in living*
> *lies not in never falling,*
> *but in rising every time we fall.*
>
> Nelson Mandela

But Nancy was determined not to end up like her mother. She found refuge in libraries, reading as many books as she could. When she could attend school, she devoured the lessons and emulated her teachers. Nancy knew she was as good as anyone else; she just didn't have quite as many possessions. She dreamed she would become a gifted singer who would be on TV, admired by everyone. She dreamed she would become a famous surgeon, saving the lives of poor children. She visualized she would become a great teacher, helping the disadvantaged (just like herself).

And guess what! She became a great teacher and a gifted singer. Though she didn't sing on TV, Nancy did make a difference in the lives of the disadvantaged and poor.

Anyone who sees such a victory is amazed; most of us would wonder how one could endure so much and yet be completely healed spiritually, physically, and emotionally.

How can someone who has been through so much devastation and such terrible experiences be on top of the world?

Then you have those who have experienced similar tragedies but are obviously stuck in the bondage of anger, denial, or depression. Nancy's brothers did not survive the hardships of their circumstances. One committed suicide; the other lives in an alcoholic stupor, a homeless bum.

So how do the survivors do it? The answer is simple, ladies and gentlemen. Attitude is a choice. The only difference between those who triumph over adversity and those who wander in the pits of depression is the individual's never-ceasing fight for resurrection.

I call this the *Me Factor*.

Here's my personal example of the "Me Factor." I am the youngest of three boys. My oldest brother, Larry, is two years older than I am. Then there's Willie, who is eleven months older than I am. We were all brought up under the exact same circumstances. We all had the same father, and we all had the same mother. We all ate the same food, and we all had the same economic status. The only difference between us was the "You

Factor." Each of us responded to our situation by taking different avenues.

My oldest brother, Larry, is currently in prison for the third time, serving a forty-year sentence for aggravated robbery. He has been in prison most of his adult life.

Willie was always the "good" boy. He made his choices early in life, and refused to become a product of his environment. Somehow Willie decided to stand for what was right. He was able to say *no* to the many temptations we suffered and he didn't make the mistakes that Larry and I did. He has been in the ministry since he was eighteen years old. When was thirty, he also became the principal of a public junior high school.

I was headed down Larry's path, not Willie's. I had a felony arrest, and I participated in actions that deserved prison time. Thanks to Mookie, my homie who was killed, I made the decision to change directions when I was 18. Thanks to Crystal, I never strayed from my new path. Now I'm a celebrity life coach and television personality and I speak to tens of thousands of people each year, encouraging and empowering the masses to experience true mental, spiritual, and physical wealth. My family life could not be more loving; I cherish my two girls and my son, and I'm more in love with

Crystal than I could have imagined 22 years ago, when I met her.

How did three brothers, who were raised in the exact same environment, turn out with totally different futures? The answer is the "Me Factor."

I love both my brothers with all my heart. Nobody is better than the other. We shared many traumatic experiences which we're lucky to have survived. Although we all had the exact same opportunities to make the exact same decisions, our choices to act on them were our own options.

We three brothers are a lot alike. All three of us are very compassionate individuals, men who would give the shirts off of our backs to help someone else, and our parents are the exact same way. We say and do many things in identical ways, but although we had the same opportunities to decide right from wrong, the choices that we made were our own individual ones. The way an individual responds to the cards dealt them is a personal choice, and that is what I call the "Me Factor."

I have trained sales organizations under the exact same principles. When I was an upper-level manager in the insurance industry, we always started out our week with a Monday morning sales meeting, discussing the previous week's production.

My top producers always had a great attitude and they shared happy stories of how they had such an incredible week. On the opposite side, the agents who didn't have such a great week always had excuses—a multitude of problems that were anything but their fault. Agents with poor production complained about the leads, or the price, or how our products were inferior to our competitors'.

As you may have guessed, every single agent in our division sold the exact same products; they all sold them at the exact same prices, while working from the exact same source of leads.

The only difference between the top producers and the poor producers was the individual's attitude. Instead of wondering what they were doing wrong, they were focused on how the company and everything else was wrong. They should have been asking the top producers for wisdom and advice.

They all were in the exact same office, under the exact same management, being trained by the exact same leaders. Why did they not all have the exact same result?

> *That's my gift.*
> *I let that negativity roll off me*
> *like water off a duck's back.*
> *If it's not positive, I didn't hear it.*
> *If you can overcome that,*
> *fights are easy.*

George Foreman

People who are on the bottom tend to point the finger at everyone else; it's never their fault. A wise person is one who applies taught knowledge and a fool is one who has the knowledge but refuses to apply it. Although many can be exposed to the exact same teachings and principles, the end result will ultimately be determined by the individual's choice of actions. This is the "Me Factor."

Instigators, Spectators, and Participators

There are three types of people in the world:

- **Instigators**, who *talk* about things happening.
- **Spectators**, who *watch* things happen.
- **Participators**, who *make* things happen.

Those who like to talk about things happening always focus on problems. As instigators, they have no problem stirring up messes, and they are always willing to throw gasoline onto any fire. Quick to talk about the problems, they hardly ever are compelled to search for solutions. They are the ones likely to be talking about how things could have been better. Individuals in this particular category don't possess the right answers, but they feel that they are qualified to point out the wrong answers.

Instigators are very unlikely to be on the inside of any major decision-making process. They are always the ones on the outside, wondering and complaining about what's going on inside. They have no desire to be in the game, but they always want to know what's going on. They love to participate in "tailgate parties." Though they are not interested in actually seeing what's going on, they're always close enough to at least hear the noise. Instigators are people-pleasers, and try to please others at any cost.

Then we have spectators, the people who watch things happen. Individuals in this particular group will get as close as they can to the fire, but will never get in; they are just there to watch. Instigators and spectators have some similarities; both are talkers with no desire to get in the game. Because instigators are usually only on the outside, wondering what's going on inside, their information is usually passed on to them by a spectator.

Spectators actually see and witness the game firsthand; they have to see what's going on with their own eyes.

Spectators can be very opinionated and sometimes even abusive. Spectators come to see two things. They want to see someone win, and, equally, they want to see someone lose. Although they claim to be loyal, they are known to turn on their own team in a split second.

Spectators are very emotional and quick to react. Even though they are not qualified to participate in the game in most cases, they are quick to criticize and judge the participants. Spectators need supervision and direction.

Finally we have participators, the five percent who actually make things happen. These are the ones who are willing to get in the game, the ones on the field actively taking part. Unlike the instigators and spectators, 90 percent of a participant's effort is dedicated to preparation for the game. They work hard practicing and perfecting their skills. They're constantly focused on winning. They are always prepared and willing to face any challenge.

Participants talk about solutions, not problems. They make things happen by addressing challenges with solutions. They are trained to ignore instigators and spectators. Regardless of what's going on around them and regardless of all the hype, they never get out of position. Participants are team players. They understand that breaking focus could bring harm to their fellow participants. There is no time for foolishness; they are focused on making things happen.

> *Let us not be content*
> *to wait and see what will happen,*
> *but give us the determination*
> *to make the right things happen.*
>
> Horace Mann

Each of you has the task of figuring out which of these three categories you fall into. You must make your decision today!

Are you an instigator, always finding yourself talking about things that are happening? Are you a spectator, watching things happen from a distance? Are you a participant in the game, focused on the end result (which is to win, by the way!) and constantly bettering yourself by sharpening your skills and preparing to make things happen?

Summary

- Anyone who looks hard enough for an excuse will find one.

- Do not let your past determine your future, because where you've been has nothing to do with where you're going.

- Speak life into your future, not death, because whatever you say, you will have.

- You must determine and be willing to accept that every individual has friends and foes. It is your personal responsibility to distinguish between the two and to disconnect from all that is holding you back.

- You possess the God-given mental ability to choose your destiny by every action that you display.

- Choose to be a winner today by seeing yourself at the top tomorrow.

- Think like a winner, believe that you are a winner, tell yourself that you are a winner, and you will win!

- Every day that you wake up is another day to *make it happen*!

> *I would rather lose in a cause*
> *that will someday win,*
> *than win in a cause*
> *that will someday lose!*
>
> Woodrow T. Wilson

It is never too late to walk into a new future. I used to think that it was too late for me to change my life because of all the baggage from my past. Then I learned why they call it the past . . . because it's behind you.

It only takes one second to make a decision, and it only takes one step to start a journey of a thousand miles. Today is your first day; now take your first step. Make it happen! Welcome to your future!

If I can do it, anyone can.

About the Author

 A dynamic celebrity life coach, motivational speaker, and television host, Johnny Wimbrey is known internationally for his record-breaking achievements. Johnny has trained and empowered hundreds of thousands of people in seminars, via television and radio, and at events around the globe.

Johnny's passion is to create success stories by helping others experience financial, spiritual, and emotional wealth. He speaks on a wide variety of issues including youth enrichment, mental breakthroughs, entrepreneurship, and finding success, to name a just a few.

His young life was marked by one of his first memories, living in a shelter for battered women. He grew up as a young drug dealer on the hardcore streets, and had run-in with gangs and the law. The death of a friend caused him to "flip the switch," and he refused to let his past determine his future.

At the age of twenty, he became a licensed insurance agent. Within six months of joining the insurance industry, Johnny received recognition as a Top 50 Producer in a national marketing agency. In less than two years, moving up the ranks from agent to district manager, regional manager, then regional vice president overseeing Texas and Oklahoma, Johnny found himself training experienced regional managers to recruit, manage and teach sales development skills.

Johnny decided at that point to become an entrepreneur himself, and he and his wife Crystal founded Wimbrey Training Systems, which works with corporations and organizations around the world. He also hosted his own Hollywood talk show as well as appears on network and cable shows such as the Today show, Fox News, Hollywood E! and others.

Johnny has shared the stage at events with Les Brown, Zig Ziglar, Brian Tracy, Jim Rohn, Dr. John Gray, Dr. Denis Waitley, William E. Bailey, Tavis Smiley, and many other great speakers, authors, and noted authorities.

His message is simple: "Your past doesn't determine your future. If I can do it, anyone can."

Contact Johnny

Johnny D. Wimbrey
Master Motivation/Success Trainer

MEMBER

NATIONAL
SPEAKERS
ASSOCIATION

Most Requested Topics:

Motivation/Keynote
Overcoming Adversity
Youth Enrichment
Leadership/Sales

www.johnnywimbrey.com

 @Wimbrey

 JohnnyWimbrey.FanPage

 JohnnyWimbrey

 @Wimbrey

 @Wimbrey

34009081R00074

Made in the USA
Middletown, DE
04 August 2016